SCIENCE Workbook

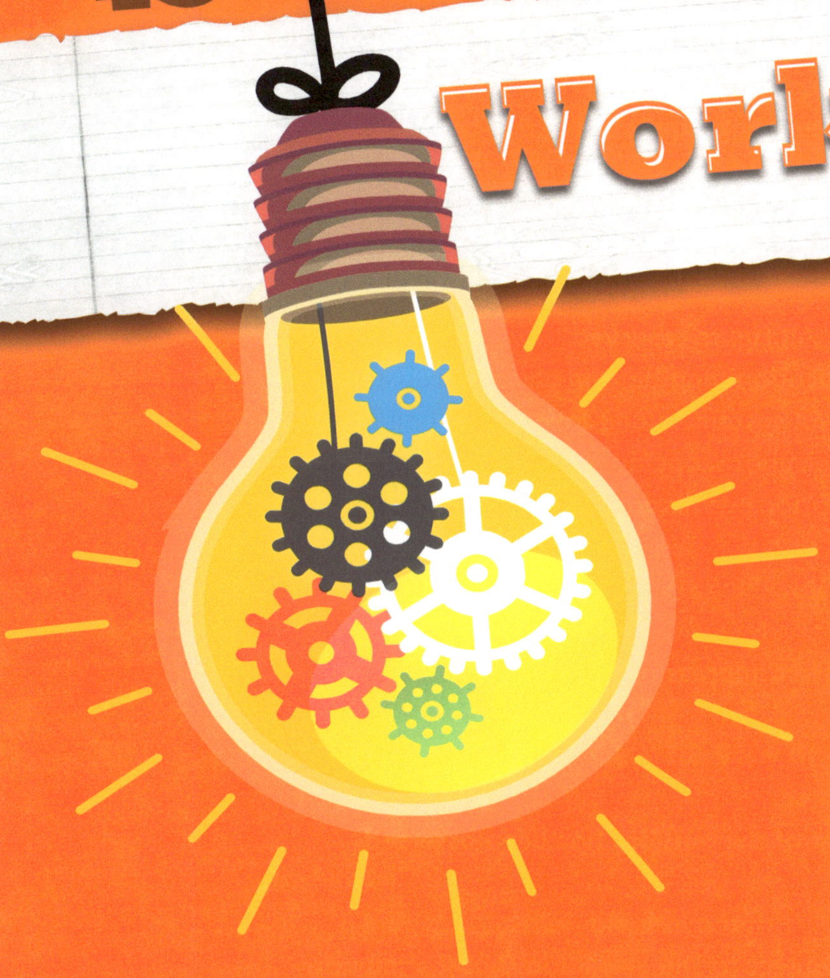

Level 3

Published in Moonstone
by Rupa Publications India Pvt. Ltd 2022
7/16, Ansari Road, Daryaganj
New Delhi 110002

Sales centres:
Allahabad Bengaluru Chennai
Hyderabad Jaipur Kathmandu
Kolkata Mumbai

ISBN: 978-93-5520-702-9

First impression 2022

10 9 8 7 6 5 4 3 2 1

Contents

Plants

1.   Fill in the blanks with the correct words.

Shoot	photosynthesis	chlorophyll
fibrous root	stomata	tap root

a.   _______________ of the plant grows above the ground.

b.   The leaves of the plants have a green coloured substance called _____________.

c.   The main root (primary root) with other minor side roots, which grow deep into the soil is called _____________.

d.   The fine, thick hairs like structure, that spread sideways in all the directions is called as _____________.

e.   The lower side of a leaf has many pores called _____________.

f.   Plants prepare their food by the process called _____________.

2.   Write T for true statements and F for the false ones.

a.   The leaves provide support to the plant.

b.   Plants such as bamboo and onion have fibrous roots.

c.   Roots absorb water and salts from the soil.

d.   The potato and ginger plant stores food in their underground stem.

e.   The leaf blade contains small pores called stomata.

f.   The leaves appear green due to photosynthesis process.

3. **Name two plants whose following parts are consumed as food.**

a.   Stem: ________________________   ________________________

b.   Leaf: ________________________   ________________________

c.   Root: ________________________   ________________________

d.   Fruit: ________________________   ________________________

e.   Seed: ________________________   ________________________

f.   Flower: ________________________   ________________________

4. **Answer the following questions.**

a.   What is the role of roots in the growth of a plant?

____

b.   What are the two most important functions of a stem?

____

c.   Explain the process of photosynthesis.

____

d.   Why are leaves green in colour?

____

e.   Why are seeds important for plants?

____

f.   How are plants useful for the environment?

____

5. **Rearrange the words to form correct statements.**

a.   the plants/ to the soil/ roots help/ stay fixed

____

b.   holds the/ trunk/ straight and upright/ tree

____

c.   the plant/ food for/ the leaves/ prepare

____

d.   inside/ have seeds/ them/ fruits

____

e.   a seed/ into/ grows/ a plant

____

f.   into/ changes/ a fruit/ a flower

____

6. **Activity time**

Collect seeds of different plants. Observe them carefully. Paste them on an A4 size sheet to make a bird.

Animals and Their Food

1. Fill in the blanks with the correct words.

Reptiles	herbivores	tears
plants	tusks	carnivores

a.   Plant-eating animals are called _______________.

b.   Flesh-eating animals are called _______________.

c.   A food chain always starts with _______________.

d.   _______________ swallow their food whole.

e.   Elephants use their _______________ to put food and water in their mouth.

f.   A lion _______________ the flesh using its sharp teeth.

2. Write T for true statements and F for the false ones.

a.   Giraffe's long neck helps it drink more water.

b.   Cows and buffaloes chew the cud.

c.   A rabbit is herbivore.

d.   Frogs have sharp claws to catch insects.

e.   A food chain shows us how living things depend on each other for food.

f.   Elephants use their tusks for hunting animals.

3. **Circle the animal which does not belong to the group.**

a. Cat,   Frog,   Dog,   Rat,   Goat

b. Lion,   Bear,   Tiger,   Leopard,   Jaguar

c. Chameleon,   Frog,   Mosquito,   Lizard

d. Butterfly,   Bee,   Mosquito,   Snake

e. Deer,   Monkey,   Sheep,   Wolf,   Horse

f. Ostrich,   Crow,   Bear,   Squirrel

4. **Answer the following questions.**

a. What are herbivores?

____

b. What are carnivores?

____

c. What are omnivores?

____

d. What is a food chain?

____

e. Why do carnivores have strong jaw and sharp teeth?

____

f. Give an example of a food chain.

____

5. Write two examples for the following.

a. Animals which eat only plants. ______________, ______________

b. Animals which eat only flesh. ______________, ______________

c. Animals which eat both plants and flesh of other animals.
    ______________, ______________

d. Animals which swallow their prey. ______________, ______________

e. Animals which gnaw their food. ______________, ______________

f. Animals which suck their food into their mouth. ______________,
    ____

6. Activity time

Collect pictures of different living things. Paste them on a sheet of
paper showing who eats whom.

Birds

1. Fill in the blanks with the correct words.

a. Flesh-eating birds have _____________ beaks. (sharp/ flat)

b. Ducks have _____________ beaks with holes on either side. (short/ broad)

c. Hens have sharp _____________ to scratch the ground. (nails/ claws)

d. Water birds have _____________ feet to swim in the water. (long/ webbed)

e. Herons have long _____________ to help them walk in water. (legs/ beak)

f. Woodpeckers use their _____________ to peck into tree trunks. (beak/ talons)

2. Write T for true statements and F for the false ones.

a. Eagle and hawk are omnivorous birds.

b. Ducks have broad and flat beaks.

c. Some birds use their talons to hunt other animals.

d. Birds have hollow bones to help them fly easily.

e. Birds can only use twigs and leaves to make their nests.

f. All types of birds can fly long distances.

3.   **Name two birds which:**

a.   Have long and pointed beak. _________________ _________________

b.   Cannot fly.   _________________ _________________

c.   Have sharp and hooked beak. _________________ _________________

d.   Suck nectar from the flowers. _________________ _________________

e.   Eat insects.   _________________ _________________

f.   You can find around your house. _________________ _________________

4.   **Answer the following questions.**

a.   Why do birds build nests?

____

b.   Why do different birds have different types of beaks?

____

c.   Why do parrots have a short and curved beak?

____

d.   Name some birds which make a hole in the tree trunk to live.

____

e.   Why do some birds have longer legs as compared to other birds?

____

f.   How does the beak of a duck help it?

____

5. Define the terms given below.

a.   Upstroke ____

b.   Downstroke ____

c.   Wading ____

d.   Perching ____

e.   Talons ____

f.   Peck ____

6. Activity time.

Observe the birds around your house. Note down interesting details about their behavior and other features. Make a small encyclopedia with all the details and share it with your friends.

Our Body

1. Tick the most suitable answer for the following.

a. The building blocks of our body.

Muscles ☐   Tissues ☐   Cells ☐

b. The total number of bones in our body.

600 ☐   206 ☐   406 ☐

c. The organ which is not a part of the digestive system.

Food pipe ☐   Intestine ☐   Spinal cord ☐

d. The organ system which transports blood in our body.

Circulatory system ☐   Muscular system ☐

Nervous system ☐

e. The organ which gives commands to all the parts of our body.

Heart ☐   Lungs ☐   Brain ☐

f. The structure formed by all the bones in our body.

Skeleton ☐   Blood vessels ☐   Spinal cord ☐

2. Match the following.

Column A	Column B
a. Skeletal system	Heart
b. Muscular system	Nose
c. Nervous system	Bones
d. Circulatory system	Stomach
e. Digestive system	Brain
f. Respiratory system	Muscles

3.   Write T for true statements and F for the false ones.

a.   Kidneys filter urine from blood.

b.   Blood vessels carry signals from the body parts to
     the brain.

c.   Our lungs expand when we breathe out.

d.   The digestion of food starts in the mouth.

e.   The muscles control our sense organs.

f.   The excretory system helps in digestion of food.

4.   Answer the following questions.

a.   Why do we need muscles?

____

b.   What is an organ system? Name any two organ systems.

____

c.   What are cells?

____

d.   Name the organs of digestive system and describe their functions.

____

e.   What is the function of the nervous system?

____

f.   How does exercise help our body?

____

5. **Label the various parts of the digestive system shown below.**

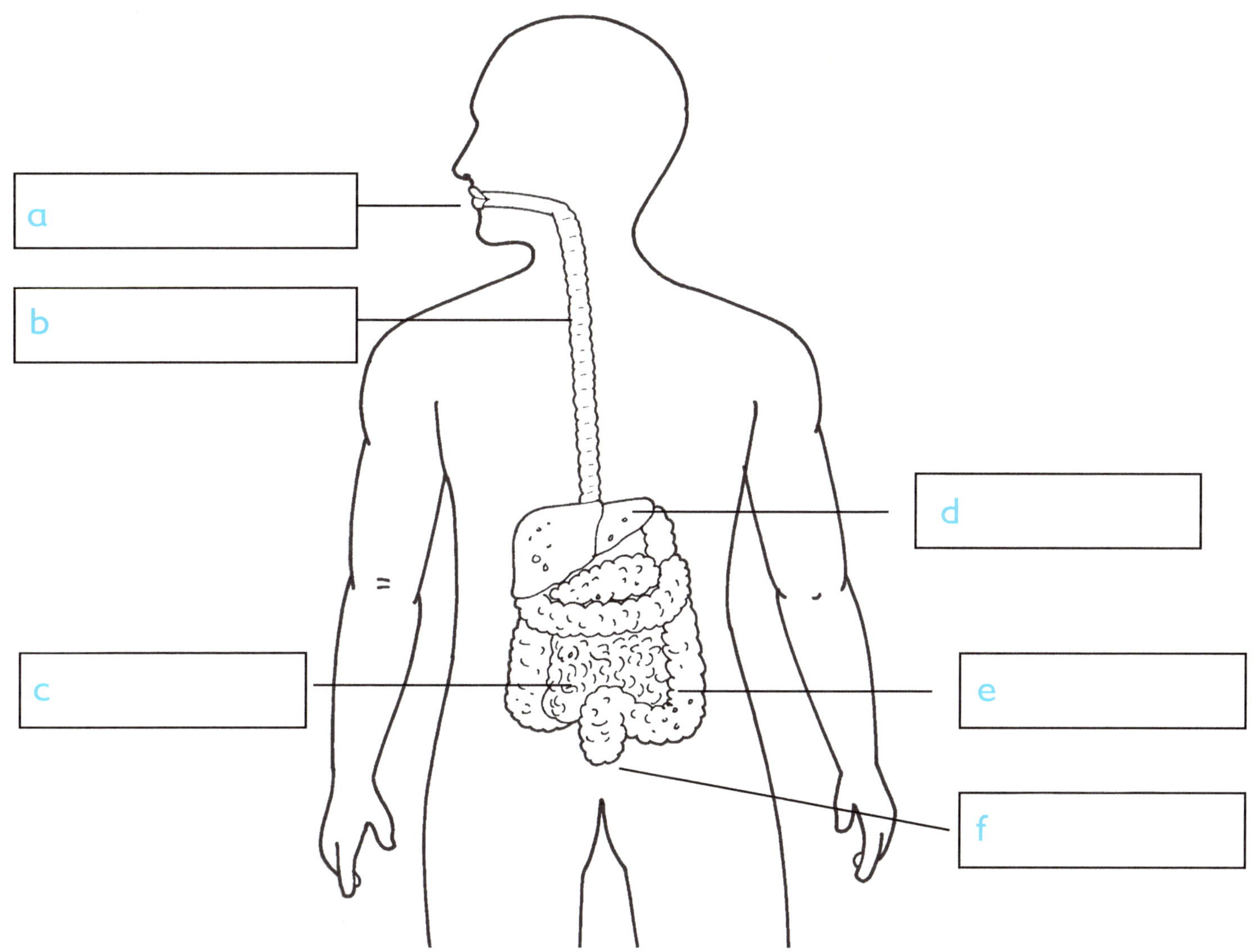

6. **Activity time**

Observe your daily routine for a day and list down various habits that are healthy and unhealthy for you. Modify your daily routine to exclude the unhealthy habits and include some more healthy habits to keep your body fit.

Shelter

1. Fill in the blanks with the correct words.

sloping	ill	tent
igloo	dustbin	caravan

a. A house made of blocks of ice is called an ________________.

b. A ________________ is a temporary house made of cloth.

c. Houses made on mountains have a ________________ roof.

d. A house on wheels is called a ________________.

e. Household wastes should be thrown into ________________.

f. Living in a dirty house can make us ________________.

2. Write T for true statements and F for the false ones.

a. The doors and windows should always be kept closed. ☐

b. A house should be well-lit and airy. ☐

c. Wire netting stops the air and sunlight from coming inside. ☐

d. Sunlight keeps the house free from germs. ☐

e. Plants around the house make the air dirty. ☐

f. Keeping things in their right place is not important. ☐

3. Answer the following in one word.

a. A temporary house. ________________

b.   A permanent house. _______________________________________

c.   An object used to build a permanent house. _______________

d.   An object used to build a temporary house. _______________

e.   Thing that helps to keep a house clean. _________________

f.   Living things which clean the air for us. _________________

4.   Answer the following questions.

a.   Why do houses on mountains have sloping roofs?

____

b.   What are the features of a good house?

____

c.   Which things can be used to keep the house clean?

____

d.   What are the disadvantages of living in a dirty house?

____

e.   Why should we let sunlight enter our house?

____

f.   What are the advantages of keeping plants around the house?

____

5. **Can you draw your house and your neighbourhood in the space given below?**

6. **Activity time**

    Take a walk n your surroundings. Make a note of the places which are dirty and have no plants. Execute an action plan with your friends to clean those places and grow more plants to make your neighbourhood healthy.

Clothing

1. Fill in the blanks with the correct words.

Woollen	natural	animal fibres	fibre
man-made	synthetic	Raincoats	

a. Clothes are made from _________________.

b. Fibres can be _________________ or _________________.

c. _________ clothes absorb heat from sunlight and keep us warm.

d. _________________ are made of waterproof material.

e. Wool and silk are _________________ fibres.

f. Polyester and nylon are _________________ fibres.

2. Write T for true statements and F for the false ones.

a. We need clothes to protect ourselves from light. ☐

b. Fibres are used to make clothes. ☐

c. Fibres can only be obtained from plants. ☐

d. Man-made fibers look dirty. ☐

e. Silk and jute are natural fibres. ☐

f. Raincoats are made using cotton fibre. ☐

3. Write two examples for the following.

a. Types of fibres _________________ _________________

b.   Man-made fibres ___________________ ___________________

c.   Animal fibres ___________________ ___________________

d.   Plant fibres ___________________ ___________________

e.   Summer clothes ___________________ ___________________

f.   Winter clothes ___________________ ___________________

4.   Answer the following questions.

a.   Why do we need clothes?

____

b.   Why do we wear light coloured clothes in summer season?

____

c.   Why do we wear woollen clothes in winter season?

____

d.   What are natural fibres?

____

e.   What are man-made fibres?

____

f.   Name the animals from which we get natural fibres.

____

5. Rearrange the words to form correct statements.

a. is wearing/ a cotton/ frock/ she

____

b. silk/ the silkworm/ we obtain/ from

____

c. themselves warm/ people/ fur to keep/ wear

____

d. plant/ cotton and/ linen are/ fibres

____

e. man-made/ fibres can be/ natural or

____

f. clean/ we should/ clothes/ wear

____

6. Activity time

Collect pieces of different types of clothes. Paste them in your activity file and write the name of their fibres. Categorize them as natural or man-made fibres.

Safety and First Aid

1. **Rearrange the letters to form the correct words.**

a. J E I U R N D   _______________________

b. W Y U B A S   _______________________

c. E S Y F A T   _______________________

d. I A S I C N T P T E   _______________________

e. D O N U W   _______________________

f. S T F R I D I A   _______________________

2. **Can you match the activities in Column B to their appropriate places in Column A?**

Column A	Column B
a. Playground	Walk in a queue
b. School	Cross the road
c. Road	Follow the rules of the game
d. Zebra crossing	Injured person
e. First aid	Do not play in the kitchen
f. Home	Walk on the footpath

3. **Write T for true statements and F for the false ones.**

a. Using sharp objects on your own is safe. ☐

b. Safety rules can be avoided while playing. ☐

c. Playing with fire can be dangerous. ☐

d. First aid boxes are not useful in a school. ☐

e. We should blow off a matchstick before throwing it away. ☐

f. Running up and down the stairs is safe for kids. ☐

4. **Write one word for the following.**

a. An underground path to cross the road. _______________________

b. It signals the vehicles to stop. _______________________

c. It signals the vehicles to wait. _______________________

d. It signals the vehicles to go. _______________________

e. A medicine that kills germs. _______________________

f. Immediate help given to an injured person. _______________________

5. **Answer the following questions.**

a. Why should we follow safety rules?

____

b. What is first aid?

____

c. Why is it important to follow traffic light signals?

____

d. Why should you not take medicines on your own?

____

e. Why should we keep our toys in their place?

____

6. **Activity time**

While you travel to different places, observe the road signs and draw them in your activity file. Find out what they symbolize and share your findings with your friends.

Solids, Liquids and Gases

1. Fill in the blanks with the correct words.

Solids	melts	Water	matter
Gases	Liquids	freezes	

a. Any substance that occupies space and has mass is called ________.

b. ________________ can be found in all the three states.

c. ________________ do not flow and have a definite shape.

d. ________________ flow easily and do not have a fixed shape.

e. ________________ cannot be seen and have no fixed shape.

f. Ice ______________ to form water and water ______________ to form ice.

2. Give two examples for the following.

a. Solids ________________ ________________

b. Liquids ________________ ________________

c. Gases ________________ ________________

d. Things that can freeze ________________ ________________

e. Things that can melt ________________ ________________

f. Forms of water ________________ ________________

3.   Answer the following questions.

a.   What is matter? Name the three common states of matter.

____

b.   What is the difference between solids and liquids?

____

c.   Explain how ice changes to liquid water.

____

d.   What is the difference between liquids and gases?

____

e.   Describe how vapours changes into liquid water.

____

f.   Explain how liquid water changes into solid ice.

____

4.   Define the following terms.

a.   Matter   ____

b.   Evaporation   ____

c.   Condensation   ____

d.   Solid   ____

e.   Liquid   ____

f.   Gas   ____

5. Complete the flow chart given below.

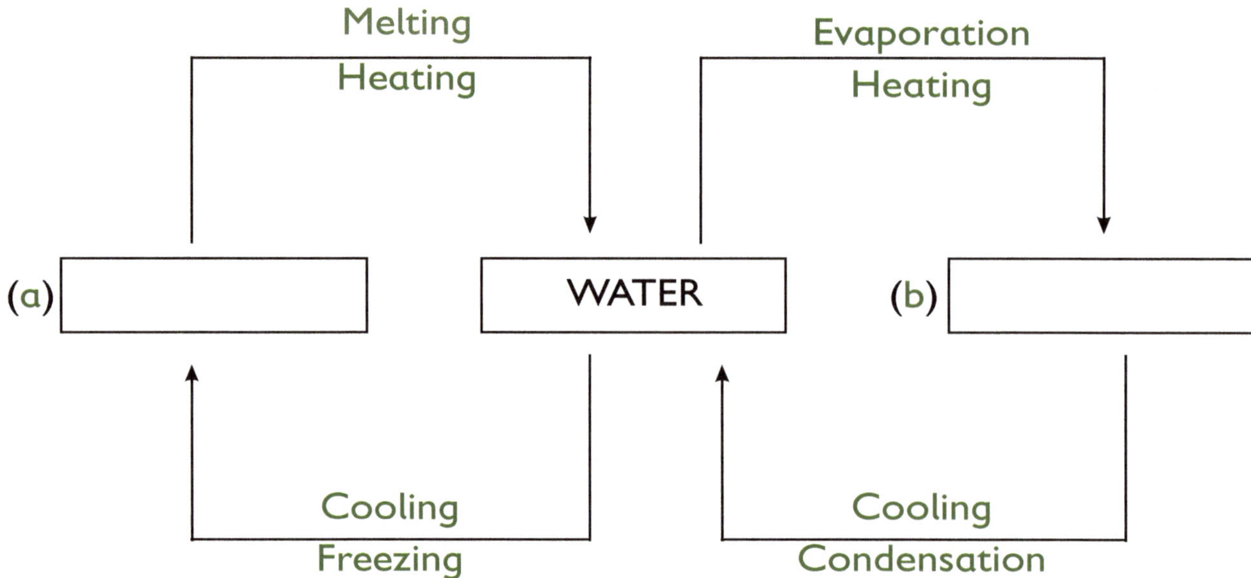

6. Activity time

Collect pictures of objects which are solids, liquids and gases. Paste them in your scrap book and write their names. Look around your house and classify objects as solid, liquid or gas.

Rocks and Soil

1.   Fill in the blanks with the correct words.

Clay	fertile	plants	minerals
water	air	rocks	

a.   Soil is important for ________________ to grow.

b.   Soil provides ________________ and water to the plants.

c.   Soil is formed by the breaking down of ________________.

d.   Humus makes the soil ________________.

e.   ________________ is very fine soil.

f.   Soil contains ________________ and ________________ in it.

2.   Write T for true statements and F for the false ones.

a.   Earthworms destroy the fertility of soil.

b.   Soil is not useful for animals.

c.   The fertility of soil can be increased by using manure.

d.   Water cannot break the rocks into soil.

e.   Soil at different places can differ in colour.

f.   The deepest layer of soil contains finest particles of soil.

3. Give two examples of the following.

a. Things that soil contains   _______________   _______________

b. Animals that live in soil   _______________   _______________

c. Things that humus contains   _______________   _______________

d. Things made up of rock   _______________   _______________

e. Plants that grow in soil   _______________   _______________

f. Two types of rocks   _______________   _______________

4. Answer the following questions.

a. What is soil?

____

b. How does humus help the soil?

____

c. What is manure?

____

d. How is soil formed?

____

e. What are some common uses of rocks?

____

f. What is clay?

____

5. **Rearrange the letters to find the names of objects made up of rocks.**

a.   SASLG   __________________

b.   TALS   __________________

c.   CBIRK   __________________

d.   EASV   __________________

e.   DOAR   __________________

f.   TUSAET   __________________

6. **Activity time**

Visit the garden near your house and inside your school. Observe the different animals in the garden. List their names in your notebook.

Take some clay and make a tree standing in the soil. Now make a few animals with the clay which live inside the soil as you observed in the garden.

Force

1.   Fill in the blanks with the correct words.

Friction	pull	less	Force
push	rubs	more	

a.   Force is a _________________ or _________________ on an object.

b.   _________________ changes the position of an object.

c.   _________________ is a force that slows down movements.

d.   Friction occurs when one object _________________ against another.

e.   A wet floor has _________________ friction.

f.   A rough road has _________________ friction.

2.   Write T for true statements and F for the false ones.

a.   The force of gravity pulls everything towards the centre of the Earth.

b.   Force cannot stop a moving object.

c.   Friction always works with the applied force.

d.   Force can change the shape of an object.

e.   Things can start to move without any force on them.

f.   The force is visible before its effects are seen.

3. **Categorize the following forces as pushing or pulling force.**

a. Gravitational force   ______________________

b. Hitting a ball with bat   ______________________

c. Taking out bucket of water from the well   ______________________

d. Throwing a ball   ______________________

e. Kicking a can.   ______________________

f. Putting on socks   ______________________

4. **Answer the following questions.**

a. What is force?

____

b. What are the effects of force?

____

c. What is friction?

____

d. Give an example of pushing force from your daily experiences.

____

e. Give an example of pulling force from your daily experiences.

____

f. How is gravitational force useful to us?

____

5. Read the sentences and circle the correct option.

a. Friction acts in the <u>same/opposite</u> direction.

b. Friction is least while <u>skiing/walking</u>.

c. <u>Force/Friction</u> causes an object to move faster.

d. You <u>push/pull</u> the pedals while riding a bicycle.

e. Everything falls itself towards the ground because of <u>gravity/
friction</u>.

f. The force should be <u>greater/less</u> than the friction to move an
object.

6. Activity time

You play different games with your friends. Make a list of ten such games and tell whether you performed pulling or pushing action in each of the game.

Light and Sound Energy

1. Fill in the blanks with the correct words.

Shadow	luminous	non- luminous
sound	Light	noise

a. __________________ helps us to see.

b. An object which gives out light is called __________________ object.

c. An object that doesn't give out light is called ______________ object.

d. __________________ is formed when an object comes in the path of light.

e. Our tongue and throat help us to make __________________.

f. Loud and unpleasant sound is called __________________.

2. Choose the most appropriate option.

a. You can see it only during day time.

   Sun   Moon   Stars

b. Organ in our body which helps to produce sound.

   Fingernails   Eyes   Tongue

c. The object which is non – luminous.

   Lamp   Candle   Table

d. A natural luminous object.

   Moon   Sun   Candle

e.   An unpleasant sound.

Soft music   Jingling of bell   Honking of a vehicle

f.   The shadows are long during

Morning   Evening   Night

3.   Match the following.

Column A   **Column B**

a.   Noise   Pencil

b.   Luminous object   Helps us to speak

c.   Non-luminous object   Unpleasant sound

d.   Eyes   Helps us to hear sound

e.   Ears   Torch

f.   Throat   Helps us to see

4.   Answer the following questions.

a.   What are luminous objects?

____

b.   What are non-luminous objects?

____

c.   What are shadows?

____

d.   What is the difference between sound and noise?

____

e.   Name all organs of our body which help us to produce sound.

____

f.   What is the natural source of heat and light on the Earth?

____

5.   Draw two luminous objects in the given space which are not man-made.

6.   **Activity time**

Go to the park early morning. Sit there and observe different sounds made by animals, humans and objects. Categorize them as pleasant or unpleasant sound.

Atmosphere

1. Fill in the blanks with the correct words.

oxygen	gases	carbon dioxide
sun	nitrogen	troposphere

a. The layer of _________________ around the earth is called atmosphere.

b. The ozone layer protects us from harmful rays of the __________.

c. All the living things need _________________ to breathe.

d. The atmosphere is made up of mostly _________________ gas.

e. The layer of atmosphere closest to earth is called _______________.

f. Plants use _________________ gas to make their food.

2. Write T for true statements and F for the false ones.

a. The atmosphere contains only nitrogen and oxygen gases.

b. Air cannot hold water vapours for longer time.

c. Air becomes less dense on higher altitudes.

d. Plants give out oxygen during the day time.

e. Air contains germs and dust.

f. Pollution is a sign of healthy atmosphere.

3.   Name the following.

a.   Which gas is maximum in the air?   _______________________

b.   Lowest layer of atmosphere.   _______________________

c.   Which gas do plants need?   _______________________

d.   Which gas do animals and humans need?   _______________________

e.   Polluted air from vehicles and industries.   _______________________

f.   The area beyond the atmosphere.   _______________________

4.   Answer the following questions.

a.   What is atmosphere?

____

b.   Why do we need air?

____

c.   What is ozone layer?

____

d.   Other than gases, what particles can be found in the atmosphere?

____

e.   What is air pollution?

____

f.   What are the major causes of air pollution?

____

5. **Some sources of air pollution are given below. Categorize them into natural and man-made.**

| Chimney | Dust storms | Vehicles | Power plant |
| Volcano | Tornado | Deforestation | |

Natural sources of air pollution	Man-made sources of air pollution

6. **Activity time**

Plants are very important for our environment. Plant a tree every month and contribute towards reducing the pollution. Practice conservation of energy in your daily life.

Weather

1. **Fill in the blanks with the correct words.**

a. Sunny days are usually _________________. (cold/hot)

b. Storm causes a lot of _________________. (damage/comfort)

c. There are _________________ main seasons. (four/five)

d. Trees _________________ their leaves in autumn. (grow/shed)

e. Winter is the _________________ time of the year. (coldest/hottest)

f. The season changes after every few _________________. (years/months)

2. **Write T for true statements and F for the false ones.**

a. Moving air is called storm.

b. Spring is an alternate name for autumn season.

c. Sun, wind and air causes change in weather.

d. Breeze is usually accompanied by thunder and rain.

e. The water changes from liquid to vapours and then again to liquid in a water cycle.

f. Rainwater can be used to increase the groundwater level.

3. **Explain the following terms.**

a. Storm

____

b.   Breeze

____

c.   Weather

____

d.   Season

____

e.   Thunder

____

f.   Water cycle

____

4.   Answer the following questions.

a.   What is the difference between breeze and storm?

____

b.   What causes the change in weather?

____

c.   How is autumn different from spring?

____

d.   Why should we collect and use rainwater?

____

e.   What clothes do we use in rainy season?

____

f.   Why is water cycle important?

____

5.   Write a short note on your favourite season.

____

____

____

____

____

6.   Activity time.

Some sports get affected due to the presence or absence of wind.
Find out the names of a few of them and discuss how wind influences
the performance of participants.

The Earth

1. Rearrange the letters to find the names of the physical features of the Earth.

a. USRCT _______________________

b. ENACO _______________________

c. TNAMEL _______________________

d. CEGALRI _______________________

e. YCNOAN _______________________

f. ONVLOAC _______________________

2. Answer the following in one word.

a. The shape of the Earth. _______________________

b. Time taken for one rotation. _______________________

c. Time taken for one revolution. _______________________

d. It is caused due to rotation. _______________________

e. It is caused due to revolution. _______________________

f. The position of the Earth from the sun. _______________________

3. Answer the following questions.

a. What features make the Earth a special planet?

____

b.   How do we know that the Earth is spherical in shape?

____

c.   What causes day and night?

____

d.   What causes changes in seasons?

____

e.   What is an orbit?

____

f.   What is an axis?

____

4.   Rearrange the words to form correct statements.

a.   the/ spherical/ in shape/ Earth is

____

b.   imaginary line/ the Earth/ axis is an/ passing through

____

c.   shows two/ different/ the Earth/ movements

____

d.   huge round/ the/ Earth is a/of ball

____

e.   day and night/ the rotation of/ are caused by/ the Earth

____

f.   year is/ every/ a leap year/ fourth

____

5.   Imagine yourself as the Earth which is getting polluted by the people. Write a message to people telling them how they can save you.

____

____

____

____

____

6.   Activity time

Take an old ball with which you don't play anymore. Colour it blue to show water. Paste green, white and brown pieces of paper on it to make the modal of the Earth. Use a globe or world map if required.

The Solar System

1. Fill in the blanks with the correct words.

a. Our solar system has _________________ planets. (nine/eight)

b. _____________ travel to the outer space. (Astrologers/Astronauts)

c. Pluto is called a _________________ planet. (dwarf/false)

d. We can see a far-off object using a _____________. (star/telescope)

e. The shape of _________________ changes every night. (moon/sun)

f. _________________ is the name of a constellation. (Uranus/Orion)

2. Write T for true statements and F for the false ones.

a. Planets do not have their own light. ☐

b. All the planets in our solar system have the same size. ☐

c. Earth is the only planet known to support life. ☐

d. The surface of sun has many craters. ☐

e. Stars do not give out light during the day to save their energy. ☐

f. Mercury is the smallest planet. ☐

3. Read the clue and name the celestial body.

a. The planet nearest the sun. _____________________

b. The natural satellite of Earth. _____________________

c.   The largest planet of our solar system.   ____________________

d.   The only planet surounded by rings.   ____________________

e.   People who study objects in the sky.   ____________________

f.   The big star at the centre of solar system.   ____________________

4.   Answer the following questions.

a.   What is a planet?

____

b.   What is a satellite?

____

c.   What is a telescope?

____

d.   What is a constellation?

____

e.   Who are astronauts?

____

6.   Activity time

Observe and draw the moon every night for **3** weeks. Name the different phases of the moon as New Moon, Crescent Moon, Half Moon and Full Moon.

Answers

Plants

1. a. Shoot b. chlorophyll
   c. tap root d. fibrous root
   e. stomata f. photosynthesis
2. a. F b. T c. T d. T e. F f. F
3. a. Potato, Sugarcane b. Spinach, Mint
   c. Carrot, Beetroot d. Lemon, Mango
   e. Maize, Peas f. Cauliflower, Broccoli
5. a. Roots help the plants stay fixed to the soil.
   b. Trunk holds the tree straight and upright.
   c. The leaves prepare food for the plants.
   d. Fruits have seeds inside them.
   e. A seed grows into a plant.
   f. A flower changes into a fruit.

Animals and Their Food

1. a. Herbivores b. Carnivores
   c. Plants d. Reptiles
   e. Tusks f. Tears
2. a. F b. T c. T d. F e. T f. F
3. a. Goat (herbivore) b. Bear (omnivore)
   c. Mosquito (insect) d. Snake (reptile)
   e. Wolf (carnivore) f. Squirrel (herbivore)
5. a. Goat, Cow, Horse, Deer
   b. Lion, Tiger, Jaguar, Wolf, Fox
   c. Crow, Dog, Cat, Bear
   d. Snake, Lizard, Frog, Owl, Turtle
   e. Squirrel, Rodent, Beaver
   f. Butterfly, Bee, Mosquito, Bugs

Birds

1. a. sharp b. broad
   c. claws d. webbed
   e. legs f. beak
2. a. F b. T c. T d. T e. F f. F
3. a. Pelican, Kiwi, Woodpecker
   b. Stork, Kingfisher
   c. Vulture, Hawk, Eagles
   d. Hummingbird, Sunbird
   e. Robin, Warbler, Owl
   f. Pigeon, Crow, Parrot, Sparrow
5. a. To flap the wings upward is called as upstroke.
   b. To flap the wings downward is called downstroke.
   c. Walking through water with efforts and is called wading.
   d. Using feet to hold the branch and sit on it is called perching.
   e. The sharp claws of a bird are called talons.
   f. To tap or hit using the beak.

Our Body

1. a. Cells b. 206
   c. Spinal cord d. Circulatory system
   e. Brain f. Skeleton
2. a. Bones b. Muscles
   c. Brain d. Heart
   e. Stomach f. Nose
3. a. T b. F c. F d. T e. F f. F

5. a. Mouth b. Food pipe
   c. Small intestine d. Stomach
   e. Large intestine f. Anus

Shelter

1. a. igloo b. tent
   c. sloping d. caravan
   e. dustbin f. ill
2. a. F b. T c. F d. T e. F f. F
3. a. Tent, Caravan, Hut
   b. Flat, Bungalow, Castle
   c. Bricks, Cement, Stone
   d. Straw, Mud, Cloth
   e. Broom, Mop, Cleaner, Detergent
   f. Plants

Clothing

1. a. fibre b. natural, man-made
   c. Woollen d. Raincoats
   e. natural f. synthetic
2. a. F b. T c. F d. F e. T f. F
3. a. Natural, Synthetic
   b. Nylon, Polyester
   c. Wool, Silk
   d. Cotton, Jute
   e. T-shirt, Skirt
   f. Scarf, Sweater
5. a. She is wearing a cotton frock.
   b. We obtain silk from the silkworm.
   c. People wear fur to keep themselves warm.
   d. Cotton and linen are plant fibres.
   e. Fibres can be natural or man-made.
   f. We should wear clean clothes.

Safety and First Aid

1. a. INJURED b. SUBWAY
   c. SAFETY d. ANTISEPTIC
   e. WOUND f. FIRST AID
2. a. Follow the rules of the game
   b. Walk in a queue
   c. Walk on the footpath
   d. Cross the road
   e. Injured person
   f. Do not play in the kitchen
3. a. F b. F c. T d. F e. T f. F
4. a. Subway b. Red light
   c. Amber/Yellow light d. Green light
   e. Antiseptic f. First aid

Solids, Liquids and Gases

1. a. matter b. Water
   c. Solids d. Liquids
   e. Gases f. melts, freezes
2. a. Furniture, Shoes, clothes, toys
   b. Water, Milk
   c. Steam, Air
   d. Water, Ice-cream
   e. Ice cube, Chocolate bar
   f. Liquid water, Solid ice, Gaseous vapours

4. a. Things that occupy space and have mass are called matter.
   b. Changing of liquid into vapours when heated is called evaporation.
   c. Cooling down of vapours into water droplets is called condensation.
   d. Matter which has a fixed shape and mass is called solid.
   e. Matter without a fixed shape but having mass is called liquid.
   f. Matter which neither has mass nor fixed shape is called gas.
5. a. Ice   b. Steam

Rocks and Soil

1. a. plants   b. minerals
   c. rocks   d. fertile
   e. Clay   f. air, water
2. a. F   b. F   c. T   d. F   e. T   f. F
3. a. Water, Minerals, Air
   b. Earthworm, Ant, Snail
   c. Nutrients, Dead plants
   d. Statue, Cooking Utensils, House
   e. Bamboo, Rose, Maple etc.
   f. Igneous, Metamorphic
5. a. GLASS   b. SALT
   c. BRICK   d. VASE
   e. ROAD   f. STATUE

Force

1. a. push, pull   b. Force
   c. Friction   d. rubs
   e. less   f. more
2. a. T   b. F   c. F   d. T   e. F   f. F
3. a. Pulling force   b. Pushing force
   c. Pulling force   d. Pushing force
   e. Pushing force   f. Pulling force
5. a. opposite   b. skiing
   c. Force   d. push
   e. gravity   f. greater

Light and Sound Energy

1. a. Light   b. luminous
   c. non – luminous   d. Shadow
   e. sound   f. noise
2. a. Sun   b. Tongue
   c. Table   d. Sun
   e. Honking of a vehicle   f. Evening
3. a. Unpleasant sound   b. Torch
   c. Pencil   d. Helps us to see
   e. Helps us to hear sound   f. Helps us to speak
5. Sun, Stars

Atmosphere

1. a. gases   b. sun
   c. oxygen   d. nitrogen
   e. troposphere   f. carbon dioxide
2. a. F   b. T   c. T   d. T   e. T   f. F
3. a. Nitrogen
   b. Troposphere
   c. Carbon dioxide and oxygen
   d. Oxygen
   e. Smoke
   f. Space
5. Natural sources: Dust storms, Volcano, Tornado
   Man-made sources: Chimney, Vehicle, Power plant, Deforestation

Weather

1. a. hot   b. damage
   c. four   d. shed
   e. coldest   f. months
2. a. F   b. F   c. T   d. F   e. T   f. T
3. a. Wind moving with great speed is called storm.
   b. Wind moving gently is called breeze.
   c. The condition of air around us is called weather.
   d. A season is a division of the year marked by changes in weather and amount of daylight.
   e. A loud noise after a lightning is called thunder.
   f. Water changing into vapours to form clouds and again to liquid form is called water cycle.

The Earth

1. a. CRUST   b. OCEAN
   c. MANTLE   d. GLACIER
   e. CANYON   f. VOLCANO
2. a. Spherical, Round   b. 24 Hours
   c. 365 Days   d. Day and Night
   e. Seasons   f. Third
4. a. The Earth is spherical in shape.
   b. Axis is an imaginary line passing through the Earth.
   c. The Earth shows two different movements.
   d. The Earth is a huge round of ball.
   e. Day and night are caused by the rotation of the Earth.
   f. Every fourth year is a leap year.

The Solar System

1. a. eight   b. Astronauts
   c. dwarf   d. telescope
   e. moon   f. Orion
2. a. T   b. F   c. T   d. F   e. F   f. T
3. a. Mercury   b. Moon
   c. Jupiter   d. Saturn
   e. Astronomers   f. Sun